Federal Tobacco Receipts Lost Due to Illicit Trade and Recommendations for Increased Enforcement

February 4, 2010

Executive Summary

Section 703 of the Children's Health Insurance Program Reauthorization Act of 2009 (CHIPRA) directed the Secretary of the Treasury to conduct a study concerning the magnitude of illicit tobacco trade in the United States and to submit to Congress recommendations for the most effective steps that the Department of the Treasury can take to reduce such illicit tobacco trade. The Secretary was directed to include a review of the loss of Federal tax receipts due to the illicit tobacco trade in the United States and the role of imported tobacco products in the illicit trade in the United States.

Accurately measuring the amount of federal tax receipts lost as a result of tobacco diversion and smuggling is difficult because these activities are, by definition, clandestine in nature. As such, any estimate of the extent of the illicit tobacco trade will have a wide window of uncertainty around it.

The method employed for preparing this report involved comparing the amount of taxes collected by Treasury to the taxes that would have been collected if all consumed cigarettes—measured using nationally representative surveys—were taxed in the years leading up to the passage of CHIPRA. At the time of comparison, time series data on consumption and taxed sales were not available for time periods after the tax increase brought about by the enactment of CHIPRA. On April 1, 2009, the federal excise tax on cigarettes was increased more than 150 percent, creating a greater incentive to evade federal taxes. An analysis of the effect of this tax increase on cigarette consumption, taxed sales, and smuggling could therefore not be undertaken.

Further, the use of survey data poses an additional set of issues. Survey experts agree that survey respondents understate the true extent of their cigarette consumption. If taken as true, the responses in the surveys we examined, would suggest that, on average, only 70 percent of purchased cigarettes were reported to be actually consumed, which strains credulity. The substantial uncertainty surrounding the degree of underreporting of cigarette consumption in survey data necessarily generates large uncertainty about the magnitude of the federal tax receipts lost due to the illicit cigarette trade. Any estimate of federal tax loss based on survey data therefore should be regarded as only broadly indicative of actual receipts lost. [1]

---

[1] See Table 5 in the attached Appendix to the Report to Congress on Federal Tobacco Receipts Lost Due To Illicit Trade and Recommendations for Increased Enforcement, February 4, 2010,

It should also be noted at the outset, that a significant component of illicit tobacco trade in the United States is the illegal shipment of tobacco products from low-tax States to high-tax states, in order to evade state taxes. This activity does not necessarily implicate federal collections, since federal taxes are uniform nationwide and are collected at the points of manufacture and import, two "choke points" in the supply chain that facilitate successful collection. However, because state taxes vary from jurisdiction to jurisdiction and are collected at the wholesale level, ample opportunity exists to transport tobacco from a low-tax jurisdiction to a high-tax jurisdiction for retail sale or consumption in order to evade state taxes.[2]

Because of the limitations noted above regarding the quality of the available data, the proposals included in this report are presented in two parts. First, we provide three recommendations that we believe, based on the results of the study, should be implemented immediately. Second, other areas are offered for further evaluation to determine whether the future data concerning revenue loss realized following the CHIPRA tax increases justifies the additional controls or rebalancing of enforcement that these remaining proposals suggest.

Recommendations:

1. Enhance the traceability of tobacco products by working with the Food and Drug Administration (FDA) on a "track and trace" system that the FDA is authorized to develop under the Family Smoking Prevention and Tobacco Control Act, so that the system can be used to the extent possible for enforcement purposes.

2. Initiate an evaluation as to whether civil and criminal penalties associated with tobacco diversion should be increased. Any recommendation would be based upon indications of whether diversion activity increased after the new tax rate became effective, and if so, to what degree.

3. Allow enforcement officials to pay investigative expenses with proceeds gained through undercover operations.

Other areas offered for further consideration are:

1. Evaluate the need to establish a "closed distribution system" by limiting lawful access to the distribution of tobacco products and imposing commercial records and similar requirements upon persons in the trade.

2. Evaluate the need to restrict access to and sale of machinery that can be used to manufacture cigarettes.

---

[2] See, for example, Lovenheim, Michael F., "How Far to the Border?: The Extent and Impact of Cross-Border Casual Cigarette Smuggling," *The National Tax Journal*, Vol. 61(1), March 2008. His results "indicate between 13 and 25 percent of consumers purchase cigarettes in a lower-price state or Native American Reservation."

3. Evaluate the need for enhanced controls over Internet/delivery sales to curb tax evasion.

4. Reexamine the approach to enforcement of tobacco tax law with respect to American Indians, perhaps by expanding cooperation with tribal authorities.

Introduction

Section 703 of the Children's Health Insurance Program Reauthorization Act of 2009 (CHIPRA) directed the Secretary of the Treasury to conduct a study concerning the magnitude of illicit tobacco trade in the United States and to submit to Congress recommendations for the most effective steps that the Department of Treasury can take to reduce such illicit tobacco trade. [3] The Secretary was directed to include a review of the loss of federal tax receipts due to illicit tobacco trade in the United States and the role of imported tobacco products in the illicit trade in the United States.

Accurately measuring the amount of federal tax receipts lost as a result of tobacco diversion and smuggling is difficult because these activities are, by definition, clandestine in nature. As such, any estimate of the extent of the illicit tobacco trade will have a wide window of uncertainty around it.

The method employed for preparing this report involved comparing the amount of taxes collected by Treasury to the taxes that would have been collected if all consumed cigarettes—measured using nationally representative surveys—were taxed in the years leading up to the passage of CHIPRA. At the time of comparison, time series data on consumption and taxed sales were not available for time periods after the tax increase brought about by the enactment of CHIPRA. On April 1, 2009, the federal excise tax on cigarettes was increased more than 150 percent, creating a greater incentive to evade federal taxes. An analysis of the effect of this tax increase on cigarette consumption, taxed sales, and smuggling could therefore not be undertaken.

Further, the use of survey data poses an additional set of issues. Survey experts agree that survey respondents understate the true extent of their cigarette consumption. If taken as true, the responses in the surveys we examined, would suggest that, on average, only 70 percent of purchased cigarettes were reported to be actually consumed, which strains credulity. The substantial uncertainty surrounding the degree of underreporting of cigarette consumption in survey data necessarily generates large uncertainty about the magnitude of the federal tax receipts lost due to the illicit cigarette trade. Any estimate of federal tax loss based on survey data therefore should be regarded as only broadly indicative of actual receipts lost. [4]

Two factors concerning the estimate of illicit tobacco trade should be noted at the outset. First, the study does not include data from the period after April 1, 2009, when the federal excise tax on cigarettes was increased more than 150 percent, creating a greater incentive to evade federal taxes. Second, a significant component of illicit tobacco trade in the United States is the illegal shipment of tobacco products from low-tax states to high-tax states, in order to evade state taxes. This activity does not necessarily implicate federal collections, since federal taxes are uniform nationwide and are collected at the

---

[3] While this report suggests some ways in which Treasury might work with other agencies to increase enforcement, the recommendations are limited to the scope and jurisdiction of this Department. It is not intended to be an administration-wide prescription for the regulation of tobacco.

[4] See note 1.

points of manufacture and import, two "choke points" in the supply chain that facilitate successful collection. However, because state taxes vary from jurisdiction to jurisdiction and are collected at the wholesale level, ample opportunity exists to illegally transport tobacco from a low-tax jurisdiction for retail sale in a high-tax jurisdiction.

We also should note that the terms "smuggling," "tax evasion," "diversion," "illicit trade," and "trafficking" are often used interchangeably, although these terms may also have very specific and distinct meanings in certain circumstances.[5] In the study and for the purposes of setting forth recommendations, we have sought to capture and describe activities in which tobacco products are manufactured and distributed outside of legal channels resulting in the evasion of tax. We use all five of the terms above, and most frequently "diversion" as it most often captures the broadest sense of illegal activity.

The proposals included in this report are presented in two parts. First, we provide three recommendations that we believe, based upon the results of the study, should be implemented immediately. Second, other areas are offered for further evaluation to determine whether the revenue loss realized following the CHIPRA tax increases justifies the additional controls or rebalancing of enforcement that these remaining proposals would address.

The proposals are meant to provide enforcement officials the greatest leverage while at the same time present the least burden on the resources of both the enforcement community and the tobacco industry. Where a recommendation might present a burden, we sought to mitigate the burden with regard to the impact on business. Our recommendations represent controls that we believe would substantially enhance tax enforcement efforts with the least burden upon federal resources and the involved parties. The recommendations are based in large part upon the long experience of the Treasury Department in the regulation of the alcohol industry.

As a matter of context to best understand the recommendations and suggested areas for further consideration, we offer a background explanation of why tobacco product diversion occurs; the impact it has on federal finances, commerce, public health, and national security; the workings of common tax evasion schemes; and the existing primary jurisdictional framework.

Background

Why Tobacco Product Diversion Occurs

The diversion of tobacco products occurs for two principal reasons: the potential for illicit gains is high and the risk to illegal operators is low. Substantial illicit profit can be

---

[5] Because the term "smuggling" is commonly associated with surreptitious importing or exporting contrary to law, for purposes of explaining the entirety of the problem of tax evasion in this report, we reserve the use of that term for only such circumstances. We use the term "illicit trade," "tax evasion," and "diversion" in circumstances in which the focus is broader than import/export scenarios and to refer to the manufacture or movement of the regulated commodity outside the legal system, resulting in evasion of the appropriate federal or state tax.

derived by selling cigarettes that have not been taxpaid, particularly since the cost to produce the product is minimal compared to the cost at which it is legally sold.[6] In terms of risk for illegal operators, tobacco is a legal commodity and can be transported and sold on the open market, making it simple to establish a supply source and distribution channels. In addition, tobacco products are an easy commodity to move in large quantities. Finally, enforcement mechanisms are insufficient to countervail the lure of high profit potential. In other words, the incentive for illicit profit outweighs the risk of being caught.

To illustrate the potential profit margin for those engaged in the illicit tobacco trade, a product that is introduced into New York City without payment of any federal or state taxes or applicable fees presents an illegal profit of $58.60 per carton, based upon the evasion of taxes and fees.[7] This translates into $3,516 per case, or approximately $3.2 million per truckload. Tax evasion can also occur "downstream" after federal and state taxes have been paid on a product. For example, differences in state taxes provide incentives for illegal operators to purchase cigarettes in lower tax states and transport them into a higher tax state for sale at substantial profit, based solely upon the state tax differential.[8]

The Impact of Tobacco Diversion

Although enforcement activity indicates there is at least limited evasion of federal tax, we are unable to estimate the scope of that evasion with any degree of confidence. Examination of data on federal tax collections for cigarettes from 1996 through 2008 indicates a steady decline in reported removals, which in turn indicates a decline in consumption. This conclusion assumes that reported cigarette removals equal actual cigarette consumption. Data on state tax collections shows the same steady trend. Examination of data from the National Survey on Drug Use and Health and the National Health Interview Survey also shows steady declines in consumption. However, the survey data indicates that consumption is roughly 30 percent to 40 percent lower than the tax data indicates (depending on the survey); this is evidence of significant underreporting in the survey data. Even assuming that there is no evasion of federal tax (an unreasonable assumption), a very large adjustment factor would be required to use survey data as a proxy for actual consumption. The accuracy of survey data as a proxy for actual consumption is limited by the significant amount of underreporting of consumption. This implies that any estimate of revenue loss which is based on

---

[6] Profit potential associated with the illicit tobacco trade is so high because tobacco products are subject to federal excise tax, state taxes, local taxes (in some cases), and other assessments such as for the Tobacco Master Settlement Agreement (MSA) (*see* footnote 8, below) and U.S. Department of Agricultural assessment under The Fair and Equitable Tobacco Reform Act of 2004 (commonly referred to as the Tobacco Buyout Program).

[7] The federal tax upon a carton of cigarettes at the current excise tax rate is $10.10. The New York State tax and the New York City tax are $27.50 and $15.00, respectively. In addition, the MSA fee of $5.40 and Tobacco Buyout Program fee of $0.60 brings the combined total of taxes and fees on a carton of cigarettes in New York City to $58.60.

[8] State excise tax liabilities per carton of cigarettes range from $0.70 (South Carolina) to $34.60 (Rhode Island). Given the extreme disparities in tax rates among the States, the potential profit from state tax evasion alone can be as high as $1.8 million per truckload. Eric Lindblom and Ann Boonn, *State Cigarette Tax Increases since January 1, 2002*, October 12, 2009, Campaign for Tobacco-Free Kids, http://www.tobaccofreekids.org/research/factsheets/pdf/0239.pdf.

consumption data will have a large degree of uncertainty.

Evading state excise tax, through interstate trafficking of cigarettes from a low tax state to a high tax state, in violation of the Contraband Cigarette Trafficking Act (CCTA) or other means, offers another area of additional potential for illicit profits.[9] Over the last five years, 32 states and the District of Columbia have raised cigarette excise taxes a combined total of 51 times.[10] The average increase over the past five years is $0.31 per pack.[11] Further, the evasion of required Tobacco Master Settlement Agreement (MSA)[12] and Tobacco Buyout Program[13] fees exacerbates the problem by increasing the potential illicit profit margins.

Tobacco product tax evasion is a revenue issue that has widespread and detrimental implications. At the federal level, the diversion of tobacco products implies a circumvention of Congress' efforts to tax tobacco products in such a way as to discourage smoking and at the same time fund children's health initiatives. Federal and state tax interests in promoting fair competition and preventing the disruption of interstate commerce also are countered by illicit tobacco trade. In terms of public health concerns, the introduction of illegally manufactured or distributed products into the marketplace aggravates health issues and contributes to rising healthcare costs, as it lowers the price to the consumer of cigarettes, so that cheap cigarettes are available to young people and to price-sensitive smokers who might otherwise quit smoking. Further, the illicit trade has been linked to organized crime and violent crime, and poses a serious risk to our national security.[14] The impact of tobacco diversion spans international borders and has been the

---

[9] In 2002, the Internal Revenue Service (IRS) conducted a study and determined that the state excise tax losses on cigarettes were approximately $1.1 billion. (This figure took into account state and local tobacco and sales taxes.) IRS, *State and Local Revenue Impacts from Untaxed Sales*, June 25, 2002. ATF indicates that the States are losing about $5 billion annually in tax revenue. Gary Fields, "States Go to War on Cigarette Smuggling," *The Wall Street Journal*, July 20, 2009, http://online.wsj.com/article/SB124804682785163691.html. If all the States agreed to adopt a uniform tax to eliminate the tax rate differential among the States, we believe CCTA cases would be radically diminished. We recognize, however, this is not a likely or viable option.

[10] Campaign for Tobacco Free Kids, *Cigarette Tax Increases by State Per Year 2000-2009 (as of October 12, 2009)*, http://www.tobaccofreekids.org/research/factsheets/pdf/0275.pdf.

[11] Ibid.

[12] The Tobacco Master Settlement Agreement is an agreement entered into in November 1998, originally between the four largest U.S. tobacco companies and the Attorneys General of 46 States. The States settled their Medicaid lawsuits against the tobacco industry for recovery of their tobacco-related health care costs, and also exempted the companies from private tort liability regarding harm caused by tobacco use. In exchange, the companies agreed to curtail or cease certain tobacco marketing practices, as well as to pay, in perpetuity, various annual payments to the States to compensate them for some of the medical costs of caring for persons with smoking-related illnesses. The money also funds an anti-smoking advocacy group, called the American Legacy Foundation. The settlement also dissolved the tobacco industry groups Tobacco Institute, the Center for Indoor Air Research, and the Council for Tobacco Research.

[13] The Fair and Equitable Tobacco Reform Act of 2004 (Title VI of Pub. L. 108-357) ended the tobacco quota program and established the Tobacco Transition Payment Program (otherwise known as the "tobacco buyout"). Under this program, payments are provided until 2014 to eligible tobacco quota holders and producers. Payments are funded through assessments of approximately $10 billion on tobacco product manufacturers and importers. This is administered by the Farm Service Agency, U.S. Department of Agriculture.

[14] The Government Accountability Office (GAO), in its May 28, 2004 report, *Cigarette Smuggling, Federal Law Enforcement Efforts and Seizures Increasing* (GAO–04-641), wrote: "According to an ATF [Bureau of Alcohol, Tobacco and Firearms] report, some cigarette smugglers have ties with terrorist groups…" GAO referenced the ATF report, *Illicit Cigarette Trafficking and the Funding of Terrorism*, July 22, 2003. See also "Cigarette Smuggling Linked to Terrorism," (Sari Horwitz, *The Washington Post*, June 8, 2004, page A01), which stated that the Bureau of

4

subject of intensive international debate and enforcement coordination.[15] It also facilitates the circumvention of the MSA, and the interests the MSA was intended to protect.

The scope of this problem will certainly multiply, based upon the tax increases imposed under CHIPRA and similar tax increases at the state level in recent years. The differential between taxpaid and non-taxpaid products is now even greater than in the past, thus increasing the incentive for illicit activity.

How Diversion Schemes Work

Tax evasion schemes function in a variety of ways and continuously evolve in efforts to outpace enforcement and operate beyond its reach. Generally, products that are introduced into interstate commerce without payment of federal tax also have avoided applicable state taxes. By way of example, typical situations include the following:

- Tobacco products are removed from the manufacturer for export, either bearing export markings or not, and are diverted into domestic commerce before export, thus avoiding tax payment.

- Tobacco products are removed from the manufacturer for export, are actually exported, and are smuggled back into the United States without the required importation entry and associated tax payment.

- Imported tobacco products are smuggled into the United States, disguised and declared as something other than a tobacco product, or declared inaccurately as to their quantity, such as when they share a container with another commodity, and thus bypass the appropriate importation and tax payment requirements.

- Tobacco products are sold by mail order, phone, and over the Internet from domestic and foreign vendors and are delivered directly to the consumer, thus bypassing applicable federal and/or state tax payment requirements.

Alcohol Tobacco, Firearms and Explosives (ATFE) has more than 300 open cases of illicit cigarette trafficking— including several with terrorist links; and *Tobacco and Terror: How Cigarette Smuggling is Funding our Enemies Abroad*, prepared by the Republican Staff of the U.S. House Committee on Homeland Security, 2008.

[11] The Framework Convention on Tobacco Control (FCTC), negotiated under the auspices of the World Health Organization (WHO), is designed "to protect present and future generations from the devastating health, social, environmental, and economic consequences of tobacco consumption and exposure to tobacco smoke." The treaty, which addresses cigarette smuggling as one of its principal issues, provides a coordinated framework of national, regional, and international groups across the world to establish tobacco control measures related to production, sale, distribution, advertisement, taxation, and government support policies regarding tobacco. While the United States has signed the treaty, the United States has not ratified it and is not currently a party to the treaty. The parties to the FCTC are currently negotiating the Protocol on Illicit Trade in Tobacco Products. Treasury has taken the lead role in representing the United States in the Protocol negotiations. The recommendations in this study are consistent with the FCTC and with topics being considered in the Protocol negotiations. Moreover, the Tobacco Diversion Workshop, which is administered by Treasury, ATFE, the Royal Canadian Mounted Police, the Canada Revenue Agency, and the Canada Border Security Agency, is a conference of multinational enforcement agencies that involves the sharing of tobacco smuggling information and methodologies to address the smuggling problem on an international level.

- Tobacco products are removed directly from the manufacturer in excess of reported quantities, thus evading the tax on the unrecorded excess quantity of product removed.

- Tobacco products are produced by unlicensed manufacturers and such products are sold without payment of federal or state tax.

Existing Jurisdictional Framework

Diversion of tobacco products schemes circumvent three primary laws, which are principally enforced at the federal level by the Department of the Treasury and the Department of Justice (DOJ). These laws are the Internal Revenue Code of 1986 (IRC), the Contraband Cigarette Trafficking Act (CCTA), and the Jenkins Act. Together, these laws provide a regulatory structure based upon the federal Government knowing who is engaged in the business of manufacturing and importing tobacco products, monitoring and regulating their activities, and ensuring that the proper federal excise tax is paid and that the tobacco products are not transferred into a state in violation of state-level reporting and tax payment requirements.[16]

First, the IRC, 26 U.S.C. chapter 52, imposes federal taxes on tobacco products and cigarette papers and tubes, and establishes a comprehensive civil and criminal framework to address the tobacco trade from a federal tax perspective. The IRC and its implementing regulations establish qualification criteria to engage in the businesses of manufacturing, importing, or exporting tobacco products and manufacturing or importing processed tobacco.[17] The IRC also requires records and reports from those engaged in such businesses. Under the IRC, manufacturers of tobacco products or cigarette papers or tubes and export warehouse proprietors storing such products pending export must maintain bonded premises as a means of ensuring tax payment. In addition, the IRC specifies that tax is determined when the tobacco product is "removed" from the manufacturer's premises or released from customs custody. There are several exemptions from the tax, including when tobacco products are transferred to the bonded premises of another manufacturer, or when products are shipped for export. The tax code and regulations also include recordkeeping provisions designed to trace the product from point of manufacture to removal, and to ensure that the tax imposed upon tobacco

---

[16] It is also important to note that the framework governing alcohol, like tobacco, directly requires the protection of state interests as well as federal interests. For example, like the CCTA, which is designed to ensure payment of state taxes on tobacco products, the Webb-Kenyon Act prohibits the introduction of alcohol beverages into a state in violation of its laws. See 27 U.S.C. 122. Likewise, the Federal Alcohol Administration (FAA) Act also respects the application of state law. 27 U.S.C. 204(a) disqualifies an applicant for a basic permit if the applicant is convicted of a misdemeanor relating to any law concerning alcohol, including the Webb-Kenyon Act; and 27 U.S.C. 205 applies the FAA Act labeling provisions to malt beverages only to the extent that similar state law exists. In view of the tax upon alcohol and tobacco, and the interests of promoting interstate and foreign commerce and fair competition through the application of the tax and labeling laws, the regulation and enforcement of these statutes is placed in the Treasury Department, except that CCTA and the Jenkins Act reside in ATFE in the Justice Department.

[17] A manufacturer of processed tobacco is a person who processes any tobacco other than tobacco products. 26 U.S.C. 5702(p). The processing of tobacco does not include the farming or growing of tobacco or the handling of tobacco solely for sale, shipment, or delivery to a manufacturer of tobacco products or processed tobacco. Ibid. Processed tobacco is not taxed. Tobacco products are cigarettes, cigars, pipe tobacco, smokeless tobacco (snuff and chewing tobacco), and roll-your-own tobacco. 26 U.S.C. 5702(c) and (m).

6

products is either paid or that adequate documentation exists to substantiate that no payment is due.

As a means to enforce these provisions, subtitles E and F of the IRC provide certain enforced collection options, criminal penalties, permit revocation, and forfeiture provisions to ensure that the evaded tax is collected and that penalties are imposed to punish violations and to deter future criminal activity. CHIPRA expanded the enforcement tools available for ensuring appropriate tax collection.[18]

The Secretary of the Treasury administers these provisions and has delegated this authority to the Alcohol and Tobacco Tax and Trade Bureau (TTB). TTB collects the federal excise tax on tobacco products removed from the facilities of domestic manufacturers for consumption in the United States. With regard to imported products, U.S. Customs and Border Protection (CBP) collects federal excise tax along with applicable duties on tobacco products upon importation into the United States except for imports in bulk (i.e., not contained in packages), which are transferred to the bonded premises of a manufacturer. TTB collects the tax on tobacco products that are imported in bulk and transferred in bond to the bonded premises of a manufacturer, then subsequently removed for consumption in the United States, as provided under 26 U.S.C. 5704(c).

TTB is the federal tax authority for tobacco, alcohol, firearms, and ammunition. As such, TTB collected $20.6 billion in excise taxes on these commodities in fiscal year 2009. Of that total, $11.6 billion was collected from manufacturers of tobacco products and cigarette papers and tubes. In addition to the IRC provisions regarding tobacco products, TTB also administers the Federal Alcohol Administration (FAA) Act (27 U.S.C. chapter 8) and the Webb-Kenyon Act (27 U.S.C. section 122) which set forth for alcohol beverages a very similar regulatory framework as that for tobacco products. The FAA Act provides for the regulation of the alcohol industry by establishing qualification criteria to obtain a permit to engage in the alcohol beverage trade as well as enforcing requirements concerning trade practices, and the labeling and advertising of alcohol beverages, while the Webb-Kenyon Act prohibits the introduction of alcohol beverages

---

[18] CHIPRA (1) imposed permit, inventory, reporting, and recordkeeping requirements on manufacturers and importers of processed tobacco similar to requirements already imposed on manufacturers and importers of tobacco products; (2) broadened the authority to deny, suspend, and revoke permits by specifying that a permit application may be denied or a permit may be suspended or revoked if the applicant or permit holder has been convicted of a felony violation of federal or state criminal law related to tobacco products, processed tobacco, or cigarette papers or tubes, or if, by reason of previous or current legal proceedings involving a violation of federal criminal law relating to tobacco products, processed tobacco, or cigarette papers or tubes is not likely to maintain operations in compliance with the IRC; (3) clarified that the statute of limitations applicable to the assessment of tax on imported tobacco products and cigarette papers and tubes, as well as distilled spirits, wine, and beer, is that imposed under the IRC (in general, three years), rather than the shorter time limitations applicable generally under the customs liquidation cycle; (4) clarified that tax is due immediately on illegally manufactured tobacco products and cigarette papers and tubes; and (5) provided that tax returns and return information disclosed to a federal agency under 26 U.S.C. 6103(o) may be used in an action or proceeding brought under the American Jobs Creation Act of 2004 for the purposes of collecting unpaid assessments or penalties arising under that Act (administered by the U.S. Department of Agriculture and commonly referred to as the Tobacco Buyout program).

into a state in violation of its laws.[19]

TTB employs auditors and investigators for the purpose of enforcing its laws. With respect to tobacco products, TTB employs chemists to analyze tobacco products to ensure their appropriate tax classification and to support enforcement cases. TTB has a Tobacco Laboratory staffed with experienced scientists to provide comprehensive technical support to illicit tobacco product investigations. TTB laboratory personnel have developed novel analytical methods and have experience in employing them for the analysis of counterfeit tobacco products and tax stamps. TTB has criminal enforcement authority under the IRC and FAA Act. The FY 2010 Consolidated Appropriations Act specifically directs the use of appropriated funds for the hiring, training, and equipping of special agents to enforce those provisions. To date, enforcement has been dependent upon the cooperation of other federal agencies to enforce the criminal aspects of TTB jurisdiction.

As noted above, the current statutory framework governing tobacco products also prohibits the introduction of cigarettes into a state without the required reporting and payment of that state's taxes. The CCTA, 18 U.S.C. chapter 114, makes it a federal felony for certain persons to traffic in contraband tobacco products or make false representations in records required by the Act. In addition, the Jenkins Act, 15 U.S.C. 375-378, requires any person who sells and ships cigarettes across a state line to a buyer, other than a licensed distributor, to report the sale to the buyer's state tobacco tax administrator.[20] Compliance with this federal law by cigarette sellers enables states to collect cigarette excise taxes from consumers.[21] The Bureau of Alcohol, Tobacco, Firearms and Explosives (ATFE), which enforces the CCTA and Jenkins Act employs federal agents, auditors and investigators, and is either directly, or through partnerships with other law enforcement agencies, responsible for identifying, investigating, and presenting for prosecution individuals who violate federal laws involving firearms, explosives, arson, and alcohol and tobacco trade.

---

[19] The tax and regulatory framework that applies to alcohol and tobacco products are remarkably similar and comprehensive. Both alcohol and tobacco commodities share a status of tight regulation and substantial taxation. The statutory schemes and related enforcement profile is consistent and complementary in establishing and promoting regulatory systems surrounding the qualification, operation, taxation, and penalties associated with the alcohol and tobacco industries.

[20] Pursuant to 28 U.S.C. 509, 510 and 533, the Attorney General (AG) is authorized to enforce the Jenkins Act, 15 U.S.C. 375, and that authority was delegated to ATFE (with FBI) by AG Order 2684-2003 (dated September 9, 2003).

[21] We note that legislation introduced this year and in prior legislative sessions would provide increased enforcement tools to address the smuggling of tobacco products, including, for example, increased reporting requirements for interstate sellers, a prohibition on mailing all cigarettes and smokeless tobacco, requiring wholesalers to obtain a permit under chapter 52 of the IRC, and restricting access to tobacco product manufacturing machinery. See "Prevent All Cigarette Trafficking Act of 2009," S. 1147 (111th Congress); "Smuggled Tobacco Prevention Act of 2008," H.R. 5689 (110th Congress). See also section 920 of the Family Smoking Prevention and Tobacco Control Act (Pub. L. 111-31), which provides that tobacco products manufacturers or distributors who have knowledge which reasonably supports the conclusion that their products are involved in illegal activity must promptly notify the Attorney General and the Secretary of the Treasury.

RECOMMENDATIONS

Recommendation 1: Enhance the traceability of tobacco products by working with the Food and Drug Administration (FDA) on the "track and trace" system[22] that the FDA is authorized to develop under the Family Smoking Prevention and Tobacco Control Act, so that the system can be used to the extent possible for enforcement purposes.

Problem: While existing required records identify whether tobacco removals in general are taxpaid, there is no existing means to tie those records to a particular package. A "track and trace" system would provide a means to determine whether a package found in the market is in fact taxpaid, and if it is not, trace that product back through the distribution chain to the responsible party so that available tax collection and associated enforcement remedies may be pursued.

Recommendation: We recommend that the Treasury Department work with the FDA on the development of any tobacco product tracing system so that the system can be used to the extent possible for enforcement purposes. Any "track and trace" system that is implemented at the federal level should be shared by those agencies that have a jurisdictional interest, so as to maximize enforcement efforts with the least cost to the government.

Explanation: Section 920 of the Family Smoking Prevention and Tobacco Control Act (Tobacco Control Act) requires the Secretary of Health and Human Services (HHS) to promulgate regulations regarding the establishment and maintenance of records by any person who manufactures, processes, transports, distributes, receives, packages, holds, exports, or imports tobacco products. In promulgating these regulations, the Tobacco Control Act requires the Secretary of HHS to consider which records are needed to monitor the movement of tobacco products from the point of manufacture through the distribution chain to retail outlets in order to assist in investigating potential illicit trade, smuggling, or counterfeiting of tobacco products. In addition to records, under the Tobacco Control Act the Secretary of HHS may require codes on the labels of tobacco products or other devices for the purpose of tracking or tracing the tobacco product through the distribution system.[23] This new law, which will be implemented by the FDA, provides that the HHS Secretary shall consult with the Attorney General and the Secretary of the Treasury, as appropriate.

The implementation of a "track and trace system" has the potential to allow tracking of any tobacco product from its removal from a manufacturer's premises or its release from

---

[22] A "track and trace" system utilizes technology and records to track product as it moves through the distribution chain. Codes on packages, such as bar codes, may be scanned each time a package moves, facilitating the ability to monitor its whereabouts as well as to trace its origin and who has had possession of it. Records are kept in support of this information. A familiar example is commercial carriers who use "track and trace" systems to monitor the movement of packages.

[23] These provisions of the Family Smoking Prevention and Tobacco Control Act (Pub. L. 111-31) are to be codified at 21 U.S.C. 387t.

customs custody to its sale at retail to the consumer. Such a system could enable tax enforcement officials, for example, to verify a manufacturer or importer's taxpayment and shipment records against a wholesaler's record of receipts, and to verify the wholesaler's shipment records against a retailer's commercial records. As a result of such a system, tax enforcement officials would be able to discover illicit tobacco products appearing at the retail level and trace the products to their point of diversion from legal channels.

A federal "track and trace" system, which would support the tax administration mission of the Treasury Department as well as the public health mission of the FDA, would benefit both agencies and promote consistency and efficiency in government. To that end, TTB has offered to FDA its assistance and expertise in the regulation of the tobacco product industry to support the FDA's development of this new system. However, in recognition of the different missions of the agencies, the significant potential for comprehensive regulation of the tobacco industry from leveraging the expertise and activities of both agencies, and the discretion available to the FDA in developing the track and trace system, we believe that Treasury should work with the FDA on the development of the system to ensure that the system can be used to the extent possible for enforcement purposes. This would further Treasury's objective to use available data for purposes of determining proper taxpayment and identifying parties involved in any diversion of the product from authorized channels, so that appropriate enforcement of the law may occur. We also note that the parties to the World Health Organization's Framework Convention on Tobacco Control (FCTC) are engaged in negotiations to establish a Protocol on Illicit Trade in Tobacco Products. Article 15.2(b) of the FCTC requires that the parties consider, as appropriate, developing a practical tracking and tracing regime that would further secure the distribution system and assist in the investigation of illicit trade.[24]

Recommendation 2: Initiate an evaluation as to whether civil and criminal penalties associated with tobacco diversion should be increased. Any recommendation would be based upon indications of whether diversion activity increased after the new tax rate became effective, and if so, to what degree.

Problem: The excise tax upon tobacco products effectively doubled as a result of CHIPRA, thus multiplying the potential profits to be gained from tobacco product diversion without a commensurate increase in penalties[25] to deter persons from such

---

[24] The parties and observers (including the United States) to the FCTC that are currently negotiating the Protocol On Illicit Trade in Tobacco Products are considering options concerning a global "track and trace" system for implementation and use among participating countries. These options include establishing a worldwide "clearinghouse database containing information collected by the Parties," purpose of which is "further securing the supply chain and to assist in the investigation of illicit trade in tobacco products." Any "track and trace" system that is deployed for tracking tobacco products should be consistent with the FCTC, and depending on the final text, consistent with Article 7 (measures on track and trace) of the draft protocol. See Article 7 of "Negotiating text for a protocol to eliminate illicit trade in tobacco products," FCTC/COP/INB-IT/3/5 Rev.1, 5 July 2009, and FCTC/COP/INB-IT/3/5 Rev.1, July 5, 2009.

[25] Civil penalties for different types of tobacco-related violations of the IRC include $1,000, 5 percent of the total tax due, or the greater of $1,000 or 5 times the amount of the tax that should have been paid. 26 U.S.C. 5761. Criminal penalties associated with fraudulent offenses relating to tobacco carry a penalty of up to $10,000 and up to 5 years

illicit activity. It may be necessary to increase penalties to balance the increased incentive to evade federal and state taxes brought about by the tax increase. Otherwise the tax increase could effectively expand the profit to penalty ratio, arguably rendering the penalties a "cost of doing business" rather than a viable deterrent and punishment.

Recommendation: It is premature to conclude whether the existing penalties are now insufficient to address the increased incentive to divert tobacco products from legal channels, without data to determine whether illegal activity has, in fact, increased following the tax increase on tobacco products. Nevertheless, as information about the effect of the tax increases emerges, it would be prudent to examine the existing penalty provisions and sentencing guidelines, to provide an enhanced punitive and deterrent profile for tobacco product diversion.

Explanation: The ability to maintain compliance, especially voluntary compliance, with applicable federal and state laws is lost if there is not a full range of available sanctions. Such sanctions must be sufficiently substantial to outweigh the risk of noncompliance and counterbalance the profits to be realized from the unlawful activity. While simple logic would indicate that an increase in the tax upon tobacco products would lead to a commensurate increase in smuggling and diversion activity, given that the motivation to engage in tobacco product diversion is to realize illegal profits through the sale of non-taxpaid products, there is no evidence to demonstrate that the existing penalties are insufficient to deter illegal conduct. Consequently, a determination to increase existing penalties should be deferred until data can be compiled as to the level of illegal activity and the effectiveness of enforcement efforts to address it.

Recommendation 3: Allow enforcement officials to pay investigative expenses with proceeds gained through undercover operations.

Problem: Currently, tobacco tax enforcement programs are funded principally through agency appropriations or from forfeiture proceeds arising from asset forfeitures in concluded criminal cases. Additional funding through the use of proceeds gained through undercover investigations would expand investigative resources without the use of additional appropriated funds.

Recommendation: Existing law should be amended to authorize TTB to use proceeds gained from undercover tobacco tax enforcement operations to fund its investigations.

Explanation: Such authority parallels that in existence for other federal undercover enforcement operations, such as those conducted by ATFE, the Internal Revenue Service, the Federal Bureau of Investigation, and the Drug Enforcement Administration. This authority permits law enforcement agencies to offset expenses incurred in undercover

---

imprisonment. 26 U.S.C. 5762. Also, under 18 U.S.C. 3571 the criminal penalties associated with fraudulent offenses relating to tobacco may be increased up to $250,000 for individuals or $500,000 for organizations. Also, 26 U.S.C. 5763 provides for the forfeiture of the unlawfully possessed product and personal property used in association with the unlawful offense. See also 26 U.S.C. 7301 and 7302 which provide for the seizure and forfeiture of property used in violation of the IRC.

operations with income earned during such operations. Use of proceeds in this manner stretches agency resources without unlawfully supplementing appropriations. This authority increases the effectiveness of the enforcement of federal criminal laws by allowing agencies to finance large, complex undercover operations, such as "storefront" operations, that could not realistically be undertaken if the undercover purchases could only be made with appropriated funds. By extending this authority to TTB, tax enforcement officers would be able to effectively pursue certain large-scale undercover investigations through the use of non-appropriated funds to make undercover purchases.

Areas for Further Consideration

As indicated at the outset, any proposals must be made with a view to establishing the greatest enforcement leverage while at the same time presenting the least burden on the resources of both the enforcement community and legitimate industry. Likewise, enforcement measures should align with, and be commensurate with, the compliance issue being addressed. Because data is not available to determine whether the CHIPRA tax increases will result in a proliferation of diversion activity, we believe that it is premature to propose more progressive enforcement controls than those recommended above. Nevertheless, in the process of evaluating the entirety of the tobacco products diversion problem and measures to address it, additional controls not identified in the above recommendations that would facilitate enforcement efforts were considered. These are areas for future consideration to assess whether they are justified once tax evasion data becomes available.

1. *Evaluate the need to establish a "closed distribution system" by limiting lawful access to the distribution of tobacco products and imposing commercial records and similar requirements upon persons in the trade.*

   Problem: While manufacturers and importers of tobacco products must have permits to operate, neither wholesalers nor retailers are subject to federal permit requirements. Consequently, the Department of the Treasury does not have the authority to compel wholesalers or retailers to keep commercial records or to require them to place codes on packages to ensure that the tax on the products they carry is paid. In addition, importers and manufacturers of processed tobacco may legally sell or transfer processed tobacco to any person, irrespective of whether the purchaser/transferee holds a valid permit. This omission in the statutory scheme has the unintended potential to facilitate illegal manufacturing activities by allowing non-permittees access to processed tobacco that can be used for manufacturing cigarettes. If the product is transferred through a third party, enforcement efforts to track its ultimate use are all the more difficult.

   Discussion: Further study should be conducted to determine whether post-tax increase compliance data justifies regulating all tiers of the production and distribution chain. Contemplated regulation would include permit, record, and other requirements to facilitate revenue enforcement objectives to validate that the tax is paid upon the products in the marketplace and, if it is not, to trace the product back to the responsible party.

Existing federal law requires that persons who engage in the business of manufacturing, processing, importing, or exporting tobacco products must qualify for and possess a permit to engage in these activities. This permit requirement is intended to ensure that only qualified persons engage in the tobacco products trade.[26] In essence, in addition to confining participation in the regulated tobacco industry to those who are likely to comply with the law, the permit requirement provides a means to then effectively enforce those laws against those who do not comply with them, through the revocation of the permit or the imposition of sanctions for noncompliance with the regulatory scheme, along with collection of the appropriate tax, interest, and penalties, where applicable.

2. *Evaluate the need to restrict access to and sale of machinery that can be used to manufacture cigarettes.*

Problem: Access to machinery used in the manufacture of cigarettes is unrestricted, and no federal controls exist to prevent the use of such machines to violate the IRC. Consequently, such machinery may be used to manufacture and distribute cigarettes in violation of the IRC without detection by federal enforcement authorities. There is currently no data available on the scope of this problem, including how many of these machines are being used for the illicit manufacture of cigarettes.

Discussion: Further study and evaluation should be conducted to determine whether federal law should be amended to require any manufacturer, importer, seller, or possessor of machines that can be used in the manufacture of cigarettes to register with the federal government to enhance federal excise tax collection efforts. In addition, we recommend further evaluation concerning the necessity to restrict the sale, resale, lease, import, or delivery of such machines only to lawful manufacturers of tobacco products. By requiring the manufacturers, importers, sellers, and possessors of these machines to register with the federal government, enforcement officials will not only know the identities of these parties, but also can ensure they are operating lawfully. In addition, requiring these entities to report all transfers or sales of machines capable of manufacturing cigarettes would enhance enforcement efforts by ensuring that such machinery does not fall into the hands of someone outside the legal distribution system.

---

[26] The statutory schemes regarding alcohol and tobacco are consistent in this area, requiring that persons engaged in these businesses obtain permits from TTB. The purpose underlying the permit requirement is self-evident, to provide a regulatory tool to ensure compliance with the laws that apply to their operations. For example, producers, importers, and wholesalers of alcohol beverages must obtain a permit under the FAA Act to engage in these businesses. Likewise, permit requirements under the IRC apply to persons who engage in the use of industrial alcohol. 26 U.S.C. 5271. While the IRC imposes a registration requirement for retail dealers in alcohol beverages and manufacturers of nonbeverage products, for purposes of notifying Treasury of the parties who operate in these businesses, no similar requirement applies to retailers of tobacco. The magnitude and ingenuity of tobacco smuggling schemes compels a statutory means to trace products to the retail level, to ensure that tobacco products are taxpaid and, where they are not, to collect the tax imposed upon them and pursue those who smuggled them into commerce. Article 15(7) of the Framework Convention on Tobacco Control provides that "[e]ach Party shall endeavor to adopt and implement further measures, including licensing, where appropriate, to control or regulate the production and distribution of tobacco products in order to prevent illicit trade." The draft Protocol on Illicit Trade In Tobacco Products, currently being negotiated, provides that "parties shall endeavor to" license retailers to the extent possible." See FCTC, Intergovernmental Negotiating Body on a Protocol on Illicit Trade in Tobacco Products, Third session, Negotiating text for a protocol to eliminate illicit trade in tobacco products, Part III (Supply Chain Control), Article 5(2).

This suggestion takes into consideration the existing statutory framework relating to alcohol stills. Stills used in the manufacture of distilled spirits are required to be registered under section 5179 of the IRC. The tax code also provides for the seizure and forfeiture of stills and provides criminal penalties under 26 U.S.C. 5615 and 5601, respectively. The enforcement interests in controlling these highly taxed commodities and their authorized manufacture are essentially the same.

3. *Evaluate the need for enhanced controls over Internet/delivery sales[27] to curb tax evasion.*

Problem: Any sale or purchase of tobacco products by consumers that is conducted through other than a face-to-face transaction provides an easy opportunity to evade taxes and bypass other reporting requirements. Delivery sales are a particular enforcement problem because the parties involved are often outside U.S. jurisdiction or are otherwise elusive due to changing Internet identities. Such delivery sales represent a revenue diversion risk because of the opportunity to ship products directly to the consumer without payment of the federal or state excise tax required under the IRC and applicable state law, and without notice to state officials as required under the Jenkins Act. Common scenarios illustrating this problem include:

- The Internet sale, with delivery directly to the consumer, of non-federal taxpaid cigarettes supplied by foreign or illegal domestic manufacturers.

- The phone sale, with direct delivery to the consumer, of non-federal taxpaid cigarettes supplied by permittees who have failed to record, report, and pay the tax upon the cigarettes provided to the Internet vendor.

- The mail order sale of federal taxpaid cigarettes to vendors who sell and deliver the product into a state without reporting the sale or paying the applicable state tax incident to the sale.

According to a 2002 GAO report, 147 Web sites based in the United States offered cigarettes for sale.[28] This number grew to approximately 790 in 2009.[29] If left unchecked, this proliferation in direct sale cigarette vendors is likely to continue given the large increase of the federal tax rate in 2009.

---

[27] The CCTA defines a "delivery sale" as any sale of cigarettes or smokeless tobacco in interstate commerce to a consumer if (1) the consumer submits the order for such sale by means of a telephone or other method of voice transmission, the mails, or the Internet or other online service, or by any other means where the consumer is not in the same physical location as the seller when the purchase or offer of sale is made; or (2) the cigarettes or smokeless tobacco are delivered by use of the mails, common carrier, private delivery service, or any other means where the consumer is not in the same physical location as the seller when the consumer obtains physical possession of the cigarettes or smokeless tobacco. 18 U.S.C. 2343(e).

[28] Government Accountability Office, *Internet Cigarette Sales* (GAO – 02-743), August 9, 2002.

[29] Researchers at the University of North Carolina – Chapel Hill completed a study of Internet cigarette vendor Web sites in January 2005. They found 664 Internet cigarette vendors, of which 46 percent were located within the United States. The location of 9 percent of the vendors could not be determined and the remaining 45 percent were located in foreign countries. In 2008, TTB and ATFE found approximately 423 Internet vendors of cigarettes; in 2009, the number of sites offering cigarettes for sale had grown to 790.

Discussion: Internet sales of tobacco products present an exceedingly complex and challenging enforcement problem because of the various circumstances that give rise to the sales and the amorphous nature of the vendors, who can conceal their identity by changing names and Internet addresses. Often, Internet sellers do not reveal a business location and may not ever possess or own the product that they sell but, rather, arrange for drop shipments directly to the consumer. Frequently, Internet sellers are based outside of United States jurisdiction. Because the differing circumstances implicate different provisions of law, and because those fact patterns will continue to change as efforts to outpace enforcement efforts inevitably continue, no single-facet approach, including an outright ban on Internet sales, will address the issue. Rather, the enforcement strategies to resolve the Internet sales issue must inherently evolve.

As a preliminary matter, we would point out that numerous approaches have been proposed by various parties to address this problem. Proposals have been made to impose an outright ban on Internet sales of tobacco products. Some countries, including Turkey and France, have pursued this option.[30] Likewise, several states have imposed a ban on Internet sales of tobacco into their states. The Attorney General for the State of Washington took a different approach, and recently proposed that legislation be enacted in Washington State that would simply prohibit Internet sales to anyone other than a licensed wholesaler or distributor. Treasury does not have data on the success rates of these various options. However, while a total ban upon Internet sales of tobacco products may be a plausible approach, Congress may want to first determine whether a less intrusive solution to the problem exists.

Our experience has shown that federal excise tax violations often accompany CCTA violations in the case of delivery sales of imported cigarettes. Because smuggling of imported cigarettes in violation of state tax laws will most likely also involve federal tax violations, efforts to reduce these crimes benefits federal enforcement as well as state interests. Likewise, to the extent that unlawful diversion of tobacco products from one state to another involves federal tax violations, a reduction of that activity would address federal excise tax evasion as well.

4. *Reexamine the approach to enforcement of tobacco tax law with respect to American Indians, perhaps by expanding cooperation with tribal authorities.*

Problem: Issues of sovereignty and the application of 26 U.S.C. chapter 52, in particular, have underlain resistance on the part of some manufacturers located on American Indian reservations to comply with the permit and related requirements that apply to tobacco products manufacturers. Consequently, while some manufacturers on American Indian reservations have applied for and been granted the required permits, an

---

[30] Turkish law provides that, "All kinds of electronic sales (Internet, vending machines, telephone) of tobacco products and cargo shipment for the purpose of selling of these products are prohibited in Turkey." Article 3(11) of No. 4207, Tobacco Control Law of Turkey. France is considering legislation that would rescind the existing ban and authorize the sale of cigarettes over the Internet. See "Internet cigarette sales could threaten Europe's tobacco control efforts," *Science Codex*, http://www.sciencecodex.com/esc_press_statement_cigarettes_on_sale_on_the_Internet, October 19, 2009.

isolated number of entities continue illegal manufacturing activity outside of the permit requirements. This illegal activity has broad and complicated consequences that are adverse to not only the integrity of the legal system but also to third parties. While efforts to resolve the issue, including consummated and proposed settlement options, have met with some success, the problem is not completely resolved.

Discussion: Enforcement of federal tobacco tax laws on American Indian reservations must carefully balance the mandates of such laws with the fundamental and vital interests of tribal self governance, autonomy, and the associated welfare of the tribal communities that all involved seek to protect. Aside from tax loss associated with noncompliance, tribal communities suffer as a result of violence involved in illegal manufacture and diversion operations. Some of these illegal operations facilitate organized crime, racketeering and other associated crimes, and violence that severely harms innocent tribal members.

Our past discussions with various tribal representatives, while not presenting a total agreement upon the issues, exemplifies the ability to work together to promote common goals.[31] Such a partnership, like that we pursue with individual states, is reasonably expected to encourage compliance and facilitate enforcement.

Based upon these premises, Congress may want to evaluate the possibility of sharing a portion of the revenue generated from legal manufacturing activities on tribal land with tribal entities for the purpose of promoting the health, safety, and welfare of American Indians.[32]

Conclusion

This report reflects lessons learned from TTB's long experience regulating both the alcohol and tobacco industries, as well as knowledge gained through engagement with other federal, state, and international regulatory and enforcement agencies.

Substantial uncertainty surrounding the degree of underreporting of cigarette consumption in survey data necessarily generates large uncertainty about the magnitude of federal tax receipts lost due to the illicit cigarette trade, which is discussed further in the appendix to this report. Promoting effective enforcement in the tobacco products trade will ensure that the appropriate revenue is collected and will prevent illicit profits and criminal activity. The recommendations and proposals set forth in this report are

---

[31] For example, the Seneca Nation, some of whose members participated in demonstrations in 1997, encourage compliance with the IRC on their reservation and have expressed their desire to partner with Treasury on tax compliance issues.

[32] Precedent exists for this type of directed allocation of revenue. For example, in the firearms and ammunition excise tax area, TTB directs revenue collected from these commodities to the Department of Interior Fish and Wildlife Service for preservation programs. Likewise, precedent for this type of proposal exists in the area of tobacco excise tax. The tribal government for the Seneca Nation requires retailers on their reservation to pay a 75-cent-per-carton fee to the tribal government, which is used for health care, education, and other services for tribal members. Gale Courey Toensing, *Indian Country Today*, February 27, 2009. In Arizona, the Navajo tribe partners with the State of Arizona to collect state excise taxes on tobacco, some of which is returned to the tribe. Id.

intended to contribute to further government-wide efforts to combat the illicit trade in tobacco products.

Appendix to the Department of the Treasury Report to Congress on Federal Tobacco Receipts Lost Due To Illicit Trade and Recommendations for Increased Enforcement

Executive Summary

Because of its clandestine nature, accurate measurement of tax evasion is difficult, if not impossible. However, the magnitude of tax evasion and the activities that facilitate tax evasion have broad implications for policy development and enforcement of existing laws. It is therefore important for policymakers to have high quality estimates of the tax revenue loss due to tax evasion.

The Children's Health Insurance Program Reauthorization Act of 2009 (CHIPRA) (Pub. L. 111-3) increased the federal excise tax on cigarettes from $0.39 per pack to $1.01 per pack, with commensurate increases in the tax rates on other tobacco products. The legislation became law on February 4, 2009, and became effective on April 1, 2009. Economic theory predicts that, other things equal, the increase in the tax rate has the potential to lead to greater tax evasion, including the diversion of tobacco products.

The illicit tobacco trade encompasses a wide array of activities. Several prominent examples are listed below.[1]

1. The federal excise tax on cigarettes is due upon their removal from a manufacturer's premises. A manufacturer underreports the quantity of cigarettes produced and then removes them into domestic commerce without remitting taxes on the underreported cigarettes.
2. Unlicensed manufacturers produce cigarettes but do not remit taxes on their production.
3. Exported products are not subject to federal excise tax. A domestic manufacturer removes cigarettes for export--and thus pays no excise taxes on them--but diverts the cigarettes into domestic commerce before exportation occurs.
4. Tobacco products from foreign countries enter the U.S. and are not declared taxpaid to U.S. Customs and Border Protection (CBP) upon entry.
5. Exported cigarettes are smuggled back into the U.S.
6. Tobacco products are transported from states with low tax rates to states with high tax rates for sale or consumption.

All of these actions are designed specifically to evade federal, state, or local excise and sales taxes.

---

[1] Colloquially, the examples listed would be considered examples of "smuggling." The term "smuggling", however, actually refers to the surreptitious importing or exporting of a product contrary to law. Therefore, only items (4) and (5) should be referred to as examples of "smuggling." The remaining items in the list are examples of "diversion" or "trafficking."

This study presents Treasury's analysis of the loss of federal tax receipts due to tax evasion. The analysis conducted below generates the following results:

- Between 1996 and 2008, per capita taxpaid removals of cigarettes decreased by 3.8 percent per year.
- Prior to the enactment of CHIPRA, the federal excise tax rate on cigarettes in 2008 was lower in real terms ($0.39 per pack) than it was in 2000 ($0.42 per pack). Between 1996 and 2008, the average state tax rate increased in real terms from $0.45 per pack to $1.17 per pack.
- Declining taxpaid removals combined with a declining real tax rate led tax collections in 2008 to be at their lowest levels since 1999.
- The substantial uncertainty surrounding the degree of underreporting of cigarette consumption in survey data necessarily generates large uncertainty about the magnitude of federal tax receipts lost due to the illicit cigarette trade.
- Due to this substantial uncertainty, the possible range of tax receipts lost ranges over hundreds of millions of dollars.

Methodology and Data

This is the first federal study that estimates the federal excise tax lost due to the illicit tobacco trade. Taxes arising from purchases of cigarettes constitute 96 percent of the federal excise tax collections from tobacco products. Further, data from Treasury's Alcohol and Tobacco Tax and Trade Bureau (TTB) indicate that smuggling of cigarettes dwarfs the smuggling of other tobacco products. For these reasons, this study focuses on tax evasion due to the illicit trade of cigarettes.

There are two broad categories of methods that can be employed to estimate the revenue loss associated with the illicit trade of cigarettes. A sophisticated approach to estimating the revenue loss would involve employing econometric techniques. These techniques are particularly useful for estimating the revenue loss due to a policy change, e.g., an increase in the federal excise tax rate on cigarettes resulting from enactment of CHIPRA. Regression analysis has the potential to illuminate how an increase in the tax rate affects consumption, taxed cigarette sales, and, by implication, the magnitude of tax evasion, holding other factors constant. At this time, however, data on consumption and taxed sales are not available for sufficient periods of time post-CHIPRA enactment to be able to employ these methods with any reasonable degree of confidence as to the reliability of the results.

This study proceeds using a "tax gap" analysis. Actual tax receipts are compared to the tax receipts expected if all cigarettes that are consumed were taxed. The difference between the two numbers is an estimate of the revenue loss.

The tax gap method has been employed in the United Kingdom by Her Majesty's Revenue and Customs (HMRC) since 2000 to estimate the tobacco tax revenue lost due to the illicit tobacco trade. In the U.S., the Internal Revenue Service (IRS) used this method in a study on the state and local revenue impacts from untaxed sales of tobacco and motor fuels.

The data used in the analysis come from two main sources. Taxed cigarette removals come from TTB. The number of taxed cigarettes removed is multiplied by the federal excise tax rate on cigarettes to determine the amount of taxes remitted to Treasury by cigarette manufacturers.

Nationally representative surveys that ask questions about tobacco consumption are used to estimate the number of cigarettes consumed.[2] First, the U.S. population is multiplied by the proportion of survey respondents who smoke to estimate the number of smokers in the U.S. Second, the estimated number of smokers is multiplied by the average daily cigarette consumption to estimate the total number of cigarettes consumed in the U.S. on average in a given day. This is then multiplied by the number of days in the year to estimate the number of cigarettes consumed in the U.S. in a given year. Finally, the estimate of the number of cigarettes consumed is multiplied by the federal excise tax rate on cigarettes to yield an estimate of the tax that would be collected if all consumed cigarettes were taxed. The difference between this dollar amount and the excise tax collected by TTB is an estimate of the magnitude of tax evasion.[3]

Consumption data from the National Survey on Drug Use and Health (NSDUH) and the National Health Interview Survey (NHIS) are used in the analysis below. The NSDUH, formerly known as the National Household Survey on Drug Abuse (NHSDA), is run by the Substance Abuse and Mental Health Services Administration (SAMHSA), an agency in the Department of Health and Human Services (HHS).[4] The survey is the primary source of information on the prevalence and incidence of illicit drug, alcohol, and tobacco use in the civilian, noninstitutionalized population aged 12 or older in the United States. Each year, about 70,000 individuals are surveyed.

The NHIS is the principal source of information on the health of the civilian noninstitutionalized population of the U.S. It is run by the National Center for Health Statistics (NCHS), which is part of the Centers for Disease Control and Prevention (CDC).[5] It is a large-scale household interview survey of a statistically representative sample of the U.S. civilian, noninstitutionalized population. Interviewers visit 35,000 - 45,000 households across the country and collect data about 75,000 - 100,000 individuals aged 18 years and older.[6]

---

[2] For a more technical discussion, the interested reader is directed to Attachment A to this Appendix.

[3] This approach is not able to account for foreign tourists who purchase cigarettes in the U.S. and then consume them. Even if there were no illicit tobacco trade, foreign consumption of cigarettes purchased in the U.S. would create a wedge between taxed sales and cigarettes and domestic consumption.

[4] For more information on the NSDUH, see http://oas.samhsa.gov/2k3/NSDUH/nsduh.cfm and http://oas.samhsa.gov/2k3/NSDUH/nsduh.htm.

[5] For more information, see http://www.cdc.gov/nchs/nhis/about_nhis.htm.

[6] See http://www.cdc.gov/nchs/data/nhis/brochure2007june.pdf?bcsi_scan_9AA99EB32CAE9A8A=0&bcsi_scan_filename=brochure2007june.pdf.

Although the NHIS data are shown for comparison purposes, the main results rely upon the NSDUH. Several reasons led to this decision.[7] First, the NSDUH interviews persons aged 12 and above, compared to persons 18 and above in the NHIS. The NSDUH should therefore do a better job of capturing underage smoking and hence provide a better measure of total consumption than does the NHIS. Second, the NHIS requires the respondent to smoke 100 cigarettes in his lifetime to be classified as a smoker. The NSDUH does not have a minimal smoking requirement to classify a respondent as a smoker. Finally, unlike the NSDUH, the NHIS does not ask if the respondent is an "every-day" smoker.

As stated above, Congress asked Treasury to review the role imported tobacco products play in the illicit tobacco trade in the U.S. The NSDUH data do not distinguish between imported and domestically produced cigarettes. It is therefore impossible to determine from these data the proportion that illegal cigarette imports constitute in the illicit tobacco products trade.

TTB evaluated other data sources to isolate the importance of illegally imported cigarettes but determined that any conclusions that could be drawn would be tenuous and unreliable. TTB considered comparing CBP data on imports with TTB's data on removals from domestic manufacturers' premises. Based on reports from 2006 through 2008, domestic removals outpaced imports by approximately 25 to 1. TTB also considered examining the legal cases involving federal excise tax diversion and measuring the extent to which domestic products versus imports are represented. However, because only a few cases have been prosecuted, any estimate produced from this examination would be incomplete and unreliable. At this point, therefore, we are unable to assess the role played by imported tobacco products in the illicit tobacco trade in the U.S.

Empirical Findings

Table 1 displays the number of cigarettes removed from U.S. manufacturers' premises for which federal excise tax had been remitted. Taxpaid cigarette removals declined roughly 2.8 percent per year between 1996 and 2008, the latest year for which data are available. Taking into account population growth over this period, cigarette removals per capita decreased at a rate of 3.8 percent per year.

The decline in taxpaid cigarette removals comes at a time when cigarette prices were rising,[8] both in real and nominal terms,[9] and when the nominal federal excise tax rate has increased from $0.24 per pack to $0.39 per pack. However, adjusting for inflation, the

---

[7] Other well-known surveys were considered but quickly dropped. The CDC's Behavioral Risk Factor Surveillance System (BRFSS) stopped asking questions regarding the number of cigarettes smoked starting in 2001. The Consumer Expenditure Survey, run by the Bureau of Labor Statistics (BLS), does not ask questions about consumption on tobacco products, just expenditures on tobacco products.

[8] Part of this increase is likely due to the Tobacco Master Settlement Agreement.

[9] Between 1996 and 2008, the Consumer Price Index for Tobacco Products, constructed by the BLS, increased at roughly 8.3 percent per year.

tax rate in 2008 ($0.39 per pack) was less than it was in 2000 ($0.42 per pack). Declining taxpaid removals combined with a declining real tax rate have led tax collections in 2008 to be at their lowest levels since 1999, when they totaled $6.52 billion. Real federal excise tax collections on cigarette removals peaked in 2002--the year with the highest real tax rate--at $9.55 billion.

During this period of time, states were increasing their excise tax rates on tobacco products as well. In 1996, the average real state tax rate on cigarettes, weighted by population size, was $0.45 per pack; in 2008, it was $1.17 per pack. Other things equal, the increase in the state-level taxes on cigarettes would increase the incentive to evade those taxes. Table 2 reproduces the number of cigarettes removed from U.S. manufacturers' premises for which federal excise tax has been remitted. It also shows the number of cigarettes removed for which state taxes have been remitted.

The number of cigarettes for which taxes were remitted to the states is less than the number for which taxes were remitted to the federal government.[10] Though this suggests there is some leakage in the tax enforcement system between when cigarettes are removed from the manufacturer's premises--at which point taxes are remitted to the federal government--and when state taxes are remitted, part of the difference is accounted for by the fact that states do not always tax cigarette purchases that occur on military installations or American Indian lands. Despite this caveat, the table shows the potential magnitude of cigarettes that avoid taxation at the state level. Finally, this does not take into account cigarettes that are purchased in low-tax states and transported for sale and consumption in high-tax states.

Table 3 displays the self-reported consumption of cigarettes according to the NSDUH and the NHIS. For each survey, reported cigarette consumption is everywhere below the taxpaid removals of cigarettes. Taxed removals can be thought of as a proxy for taxed purchases. This implies that from 2002 through 2007, on average, only 70 percent and 60 percent--depending on the survey used[11]--of purchased cigarettes were reported to be consumed.

Two behaviors could account for this discrepancy. Consumers could underreport the number of cigarettes they consume, and consumers could stockpile cigarettes for future use. The latter is implausible because of the sheer magnitude of the storage activity-- roughly 100 billion cigarettes *in net* would have to be stockpiled--that would be taking place for a product that decays in quality over a relatively short period of time.

Underreporting is a plausible explanation. Underreporting of cigarette consumption in survey data occurs in two ways: (1) respondents answer that they do not smoke when, in fact, they do smoke and (2) respondents who smoke underreport the amount of cigarettes

---

[10] 1999 appears to be an outlier.

[11] The differential is almost surely due to the fact that the NSDUH surveys people 12 years of age and older and the NHIS surveys people 18 years of age and older.

they consume. Researchers in the field acknowledge the prevalence of underreporting of cigarette consumption in survey data.[12]

In papers that examine cigarette diversions from low-tax to high-tax states, underreporting of consumption is not necessarily a major hindrance to estimating the effects of a tax increase on smuggling. However, in a tax gap analysis, issues of underreporting loom large in determining the magnitude of tax revenue lost due to the illicit tobacco trade.

Table 4 reports the tax revenue that would be raised if all reported consumed cigarettes were taxed. Since reported consumption is less than taxed removals, the estimate for the revenue loss is negative. The interpretation that necessarily follows this estimate is that there is "negative" tax evasion; between 2002 and 2007, manufacturers remitted, in aggregate, at least $2 billion more per year in federal excise taxes than is required of them. This is implausible and highlights how underreporting of cigarette consumption in survey data directly impacts the estimates of tax evasion.

The degree of underreporting of cigarette consumption, how the magnitude of underreporting has changed over time in the face of increasing tax rates and social stigma associated with tobacco use, and how underreporting is correlated with observable characteristics of survey respondents, e.g., age and sex, are unresolved empirical questions. Thus we are only able to see how different degrees of underreporting impact the estimates of tax evasion. These estimates are presented in Table 5.

Each column is constructed in the following manner. For a given level of underreporting, say x percent, the aggregate consumption estimates from the NSDUH survey shown in Table 3 are multiplied by $1+0.01x$. This new estimated consumption is then multiplied by the federal excise tax rate to estimate the federal tax receipts that would be expected if all cigarettes consumed were taxed. The actual tax receipts are subtracted from this amount to yield the estimate of the revenue loss.

Finally, three intuitive results regarding tax loss and underreporting should be mentioned. Holding reported consumption fixed, the estimated tax loss increases as either the tax rate increases or the degree of underreporting increases. Further, holding reported consumption fixed, the increase in the tax loss associated with an increase in tax rate is greater for higher degrees of underreporting.[13]

---

[12] "Unfortunately, it is well known that respondents consistently understate the quantity of tobacco consumed when responding to such surveys." World Bank Economics of Tobacco Toolkit Tool 7, "Understand, Measure, and Combat Tobacco Smuggling."

[13] These results are shown in Attachment A to this Appendix.

Table 1: Taxed Cigarettes and Federal Excise Tax Receipts

Year	Taxed Cigarettes Removed (millions)	Cigarettes Removed per Capita	Federal Excise Tax Rate per 1,000 Cigarettes ($s)	Federal Excise Receipts ($ millions)	Real Federal Excise Tax Rate per 1,000 Cigarettes ($s)	Real Federal Excise Receipts ($ millions)
1996	486,937	1,808	12.00	5,843	15.67	7,629
1997	485,761	1,782	12.00	5,829	15.40	7,479
1998	460,485	1,669	12.00	5,526	15.22	7,010
1999	434,564	1,557	12.00	5,215	15.00	6,520
2000	433,178	1,535	17.00	7,364	20.80	9,012
2001	426,787	1,497	17.00	7,255	20.34	8,683
2002	415,962	1,446	19.50	8,111	22.96	9,552
2003	399,776	1,378	19.50	7,796	22.48	8,987
2004	397,655	1,358	19.50	7,754	21.86	8,693
2005	381,013	1,289	19.50	7,430	21.15	8,060
2006	380,681	1,276	19.50	7,423	20.49	7,799
2007	361,753	1,201	19.50	7,054	19.92	7,205
2008	346,419	1,139	19.50	6,755	19.50	6,755

Source: Cigarette removals come from TTB. Population data are the Intercensal Population Estimates from the U.S. Census Bureau. The federal tax receipts are calculated by multiplying the removed number of cigarettes by the tax per cigarette. The federal excise tax rate and the excise tax receipts were adjusted for inflation using the GDP implicit price deflator and are reported in 2008 constant dollars.

Table 2: State Taxpaid Cigarettes vs. Federal Taxpaid Cigarettes

Year	Average State Tax Rate per 1,000 Cigarettes ($s)	Cigarettes Removed Taxpaid, State	Cigarettes Removed Taxpaid, Federal	Difference (State - Federal)	Difference (%)
1996	22.38	459,462	486,937	-27,475	-5.6
1997	22.44	460,910	485,761	-24,851	-5.1
1998	22.85	455,110	460,485	-5,375	-1.2
1999	28.01	439,456	434,564	4,892	1.1
2000	30.07	428,100	433,178	-5,078	-1.2
2001	29.44	414,544	426,787	-12,243	-2.9
2002	32.55	408,698	415,962	-7,264	-1.7
2003	41.48	386,726	399,776	-13,050	-3.3
2004	43.25	378,438	397,655	-19,217	-4.8
2005	45.75	371,808	381,013	-9,205	-2.4
2006	47.88	362,016	380,681	-18,665	-4.9
2007	52.45	352,944	361,753	-8,809	-2.4
2008	58.55	334,740	346,419	-11,679	-3.4

Source: Values are in millions of cigarettes. Federal taxpaid cigarette removals come from TTB. State tax rates come from Orzechowski and Walker, "The Tax Burden on Tobacco," Vol. 43(2008), pp.15-6. The rates are weighted by the state's population size and are adjusted for inflation using the GDP implicit price deflator. Dollar values are reported in 2008 constant dollars. The population data are the Intercensal population estimates from the U.S. Census Bureau. State taxpaid cigarette removals come from Orzechowski and Walker, pp. 33-4.

Table 3: Self-reported Consumption of Cigarettes

Year	Cigarettes Removed Taxpaid	Reported Consumption (NSDUH)	Reported Consumption/Taxpaid Cigarettes (NSDUH) (%)	Reported Consumption (NHIS)	Reported Consumption/Taxpaid Cigarettes (NHIS) (%)
2002	415,962	279,587	67.2	258,261	62.1
2003	399,776	276,582	69.2	241,983	60.5
2004	397,655	285,614	71.8	205,312	51.6
2005	381,013	261,709	68.7	234,573	61.6
2006	380,681	272,799	71.7	234,038	61.5
2007	361,753	257,950	71.3	217,258	60.1

Source: Values are millions of cigarettes. Federal taxpaid cigarette removals come from TTB. The consumption data come from two sources: the National Survey on Drug Use and Health (NSDUH) and the National Health Interview Survey (NHIS).

Table 4: Federal Tobacco Excise Tax Revenue Lost due to Tax Evasion

Year	Potential Federal Excise Receipts	Actual Federal Excise Tax Receipts	Revenue Loss due to Tax Evasion	Potential Real Federal Excise Receipts	Actual Real Federal Excise Tax Receipts	Real Revenue Loss due to Tax Evasion
2002	5,452	8,111	-2,659	6,421	9,552	-3,131
2003	5,393	7,796	-2,403	6,218	8,987	-2,769
2004	5,569	7,754	-2,185	6,244	8,693	-2,449
2005	5,103	7,430	-2,327	5,536	8,060	-2,524
2006	5,320	7,423	-2,103	5,589	7,799	-2,210
2007	5,030	7,054	-2,024	5,137	7,205	-2,068

Notes: Dollar values are in millions. Potential and actual excise tax receipts were adjusted for inflation using the GDP implicit price deflator and are reported in 2008 constant dollars. Potential federal excise receipts are calculated by multiplying the excise tax rate by reported cigarette consumption amounts from the NSDUH data. The consumption data are not adjusted to reflect underreporting.

Table 5: Federal Excise Tax Revenue Lost due to Tax Evasion

Panel A: Nominal Dollars

			Degree of Underreporting			
Year	20%	30%	40%	50%	60%	70%
2002	-1,569	-1,023	-478	67	612	1,157
2003	-1,324	-785	-245	294	833	1,373
2004	-1,071	-514	43	600	1,157	1,714
2005	-1,306	-796	-285	225	735	1,246
2006	-1,039	-508	24	556	1,088	1,620
2007	-1,018	-515	-12	491	994	1,497

Panel B: 2008 Constant Dollars

			Degree of Underreporting			
Year	20%	30%	40%	50%	60%	70%
2002	-1,847	-1,205	-563	79	721	1,363
2003	-1,526	-904	-282	340	961	1,583
2004	-1,201	-576	48	672	1,297	1,921
2005	-1,416	-863	-309	244	798	1,352
2006	-1,092	-534	25	584	1,143	1,702
2007	-1,040	-526	-13	501	1,015	1,529

Notes: Potential federal excise receipts are calculated by multiplying the excise tax rate by reported cigarette consumption amounts from the NSDUH data. After the consumption data are aggregated, they are adjusted for underreporting by the amount indicated in the column heading. Potential and actual excise tax receipts were adjusted for inflation using the GDP implicit price deflator.

Conclusion

CHIPRA increased the federal excise tax on cigarettes from $0.39 per pack to $1.01 per pack, with commensurate increases in the tax rates on other tobacco products. Economic theory predicts that, other things equal, the increase in the tax rate has the potential to lead to greater tax evasion, including smuggling of tobacco products. Once data from 2009 and 2010 become available, it may be possible to estimate the extent of revenue loss following the tax increase. The magnitude of tax evasion and the activities that facilitate tax evasion have broad implications for policy development and enforcement of existing laws.

Congress directed Treasury to conduct a study reviewing the loss of Federal tax receipts due to illicit tobacco trade in the United States. A ``tax gap'' method of analysis was employed to estimate tax evasion in the cigarette market, comparing actual tax collections from TTB data and the tax receipts that would be expected if all consumed cigarettes--estimated using the NSDUH, a nationally representative survey--were taxed.

Issues of underreporting loom large in determining the magnitude of tax revenue lost due to the illicit tobacco trade. Reported consumption averages about 70 percent of taxed cigarette removals between 2002 and 2007. Absent making any adjustment for underreporting, the estimated tax evasion is negative; if this were true, manufacturers would be remitting more excise taxes to the Treasury than were owed. This result is implausible. Thus some factor of underreporting must be used. The substantial uncertainty surrounding the degree of underreporting of cigarette consumption in survey data necessarily generates large uncertainty about the magnitude of federal tax receipts lost due to the illicit cigarette trade.

Attachment A to the Appendix

Let the U.S. population in age-sex cell i in year t be N_{it}. The proportion of individuals in this cell who report themselves as smokers is $\hat{\theta}_{it}$. So, the number of smokers in this cell is $\hat{\theta}_{it} \cdot N_{it}$. The number of cigarettes consumed by people in this cell is calculated by multiplying the average daily number of cigarettes reported to be consumed, $\hat{Cigs}_{it}$, by the number of days in the year, $Days_t$, i.e., $\hat{Cigs}_{it} \cdot Days_t$. Multiplying the number of cigarettes consumed by the number of people and then summing over the age-sex groups will yield the estimated total number of cigarettes reported to be consumed in the U.S. in year t:

$$\hat{Q}_t \equiv \sum_i \left(\left(\hat{Cigs}_{it} \cdot Days_t \right) \times \left(\hat{\theta}_{it} \cdot N_{it} \right) \right). \tag{1}$$

Let C_t be total actual cigarette consumption in the U.S. in year t. Let Q_t be the number of cigarettes that were tax paid in year t, and let S_t be the number of cigarettes that were *not* tax paid, i.e., "smuggled" cigarettes, in year t. Cigarette consumption is equal to the sum of tax paid and non-tax paid cigarettes:

$$C_t \equiv Q_t + S_t. \tag{2}$$

Let U_t be the number of cigarettes not *reported* consumed but that were actually consumed in the U.S. in year t. Cigarette consumption is equal to the sum of reported and non-reported cigarette consumption:

$$C_t \equiv \hat{Q}_t + U_t. \tag{3}$$

$\hat{Q}_t$ is observed in survey data, but U_t is not (by definition).

Congress asked for Treasury to determine the magnitude of the revenue lost due to smoking. Letting the excise tax rate on cigarettes be τ_t, this value is $\tau_t \cdot S_t$. Solving equation (2) for S_t and substituting in the expression, the revenue loss due to smuggling is

$$\tau_t \cdot S_t \equiv \tau_t \cdot \left(C_t - Q_t \right) = \tau_t \cdot C_t - \tau_t \cdot Q_t. \tag{4}$$

The first term is the tax revenue that would be raised if all cigarettes that were consumed were taxed. The second term is actual tax revenue raised.

Based on equation (4), in order to estimate the revenue lost due to smuggling, we need an accurate estimate of total consumption, C_t. Substituting equation (3) into (4), we have the revenue loss equals

$$\tau_t \cdot \left(\hat{Q}_t + U_t - Q_t\right) = \tau_t \cdot \left(\hat{Q}_t - Q_t\right) + \tau_t \cdot U_t. \tag{5}$$

Note that the first term on the right-hand side contains variables that are observed in the data; again, U_t is unobserved. If there is no under-reporting of cigarette consumption, i.e., $U_t = 0$, then we will have an accurate estimate of the revenue lost due to smuggling. However, holding the tax rate fixed, the greater is the degree of underreporting, the greater is the estimated revenue loss. Further, if higher tax rates are associated with higher rates of underreporting of cigarette consumption, the estimates of revenue loss will be even larger. Finally, in the data, reported consumption is less than tax paid purchases $\left(\hat{Q}_t < Q_t\right)$, which makes getting an accurate handle on the degree of underreporting even more important.

One can attempt to correct for underreporting by adjusting the reported consumption data by a correction factor, $\alpha > 1$. One multiplies reported consumption by the correction factor to get an estimate of actual consumption. Call this $\hat{C}_t$, so that

$$\hat{C}_t \equiv \alpha \cdot \hat{Q}_t. \tag{6}$$

Plugging this into equation (4), the estimated revenue loss due to smuggling is

$$\tau_t \cdot \left(\hat{C}_t - Q_t\right) = \tau_t \cdot \hat{C}_t - \tau_t \cdot Q_t = \alpha \cdot \tau_t \cdot \hat{Q}_t - \tau_t \cdot Q_t. \tag{7}$$

The value of the correction factor matters a great deal in determining the revenue lost due to smuggling. The change in the revenue loss given a one unit change in the correction factor is

$$\frac{\partial\left(\tau_t \cdot \left(\hat{C}_t - Q_t\right)\right)}{\partial \alpha} = \tau_t \cdot \hat{Q}_t > 0. \tag{8}$$

All else equal, increasing the correction factor leads to a greater estimate of revenue loss. Further, holding reported consumption fixed, the increase in the tax loss associated with an increase in the underreporting rate is greater the higher is the tax rate:

$$\frac{\partial^2\left(\tau_t \cdot \left(\hat{C}_t - Q_t\right)\right)}{\partial \alpha \partial \tau_t} = \hat{Q}_t > 0. \tag{9}$$

2